Traditions Around The World
Jewelry

by Louise Tythacott

Thomson Learning

Traditions Around The World

Body Decoration

Costumes

Dance

Games

Jewelry

Masks

Consultant: Anthony Shelton, Keeper of Non-Western Art and Anthropology, Royal Pavilion Art Gallery and Museums, Brighton, East Sussex, England.

COVER: A Bedouin woman wearing traditional jewelry.

First published in the United States in 1995 by
Thomson Learning
115 Fifth Avenue
New York, NY 10003

First published in Great Britain in 1994 by Wayland (Publishers) Ltd.

Library of Congress Cataloging-in-Publication Data
Tythacott, Louise.
  Jewelry / by Louise Tythacott
    p. cm.—(Traditions around the world)
  Includes bibliographical references and index.
  ISBN 1-56847-229-3
  1. Jewelry making—Juvenile literature. 2. Ethnic jewelry—Juvenile literature. [1. Jewelry. 2. Handicraft.] I. Title.
II. Series.
TT212.T98   1995
391'.7—dc20   94-32637

Printed in Italy

Picture acknowledgments:

The publishers wish to thank the following for providing the photographs for this book: British Museum 6, 7, 9, 10 – 11; Chapel Studios 28 (Zul Mukhida); Sue Cunningham 22, 24, 25, 38; Robert Harding Picture library 4–5 (top), 12, 18, 26, 44; Life File 11 (0. Svyatolavsky); Tony Stone Worldwide 2 (both, left N. DeVore), 4–5 (bottom, D. Torckler), 27 (N. DeVore), 30 (H. Kavanagh), 32, 37, 42 (D. Torckler); Wayland Picture Library 5(top right), 33; Werner Forman Archive 1 (Museum of the American Indian, USA), 4 (bottom left), 14–15 (Plains Indians Museum, USA), 15 (Alaska Gallery of Eskimo Art), 21 (Museum of the American Indian), 23, 29 (Schindler Collection, New York), 34–5, 36, 40–41, 43 (Museum of Mankind, UK); Zefa Picture Library 16–17; Laura Zito *cover*.

The artwork is by Peter Bull.

Contents

Jewelry around the world

ALASKA

NORTH

CANADA

AMERICA

U S A

MEXICO

HAWAII

CENTRAL
AMERICA

COLOMBIA

PERU

MARQUESAS
ISLANDS

SOUTH

AMERICA

**The foot of Nana Owusu
Sampa III, an Ashanti king
from Ghana** ▼

◄ Bulgarian folksingers wearing traditional jewelry

▲ A woman from the Philippines. Her beads are worn to show her wealth.

◄ A dancer from Port Moresby, Papua New Guinea

5

Introduction

Jewelry is one of the oldest forms of decorative art. A necklace was discovered in Arpachiya (modern Iraq) that was made over 7,000 years ago, and a pendant was found in Africa that is believed to be about 15,000 years old. Jewelry is also one of the most modern and inventive art forms. Nowadays, among the Wahgi people in Papua New Guinea, bubble-gum wrappers, bottle tops, and sardine cans are used to adorn the body.

Jewelry is made and worn for many purposes: to show power, wealth, and status; for protection and healing; to show strength and courage; to send messages; or simply to make the wearer look more beautiful. Among certain peoples in Africa, women are considered beautiful only when they wear thousands of colorful glass beads around their necks. On the other hand, other peoples in Africa are known to "decorate" their women to make them look ugly, so that they will not be stolen by other peoples and used as slaves.

Jewelry can be created from many things. In cultures where gold, silver, and precious stones are rare and expensive, jewelry made from these materials shows importance or wealth. However, in other cultures different materials are valued, and jewelry is made from shells, bones, teeth, feathers, hair, and even newspaper, plastic, or old tin.

Around the world, jewelry is worn by both men and women. In Europe and North America, women generally wear more decoration than men, but in other parts of the world it is often the men who are the most colorful and ornate.

Jewelry can be either functional, such as a brooch or pin to fasten clothing, or seen as an art form. Modern artists create "designer" jewelry, and some Native American groups sell their bracelets and necklaces in art galleries.

However it has been made, and whatever it has been made for, jewelry has played an important part in the lives of men and women for centuries and will surely continue to do so for centuries to come.

◄ **Main picture: This court jewelry is from Ur, Sumer, and is about 4,500 years old.**

◄ **Far left: The ancient Egyptians wore much jewelry. This detail of a wall painting shows female musicians wearing gold earrings, bangles, and amulets. It is from the tomb of Nebamun at Thebes, built about 3,500 years ago.**

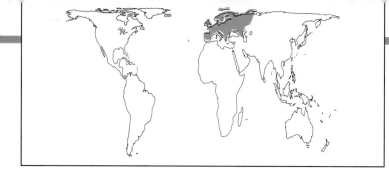

Europe

Today in Europe, many people wear jewelry as a form of decoration. Anyone can wear jewels, from children to old people, but men tend to wear less decoration than women. Nowadays it is possible to buy many different types of jewelry, from cheap plastic trinkets to the expensive gold and silver jewels sold in exclusive shops. Decoration can be worn all over the body, but people generally wear ornaments on their ears and fingers and around their necks and wrists.

Jewelry is even seen as an art form: famous designers, such as Fabergé, have created pieces that are considered to be modern art. The surrealist painter Salvador Dali, for example, designed earrings in the shape of telephone receivers and rings that looked like snails. Modern designers use a variety of materials to create their jewelry. Besides precious metals, they use plastic and acrylic, and some even paint chicken and animal bones with enamel.

People have been wearing jewelry in Europe for thousands of years. Hoards of Bronze and Iron Age brooches, pins, and arm rings have been found, mostly in burial sites. The Celts made many different types of jewelry, but the most common ornament was the brooch. This was worn on one or both shoulders and was used to fasten cloaks.

These early pieces probably had magical functions, too – they may have served as amulets to protect the wearer from harm. The Celts also put jewelry on the bodies of the dead, so most of the ancient pieces now in museums have

▲ **A dragon-shaped brooch from early Britain. This dates from the second century A.D. and is made of bronze and enamel.**

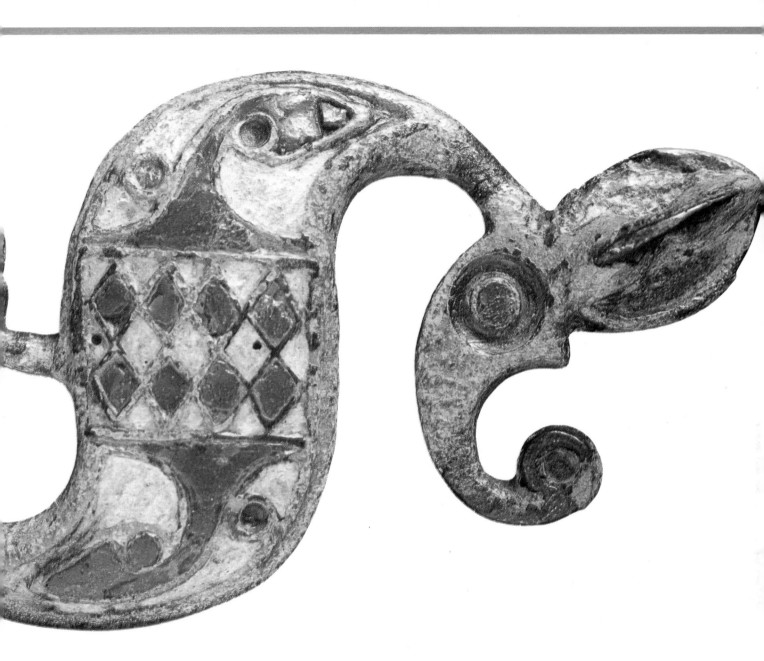

come from graves. The Anglo-Saxons and Vikings made many brooches, pins, and necklaces from silver and gold and buried them with the dead.

By the mid-sixteenth century, Spain was the richest country in Europe because of all the gold and precious stones that arrived there from Central and South America. The leading goldsmiths and jewelers of the time moved from court to court, from the kingdoms of northern Europe and Britain down to Italy and Spain. At this time, jewels were worn as much by men as by women, to show their status in society.

The kings and queens of Europe had the finest jewels of all. Today, royal families in Britain, Sweden, and Denmark all have wonderful crown jewels that have been collected over hundreds of years. Some are still worn for public ceremonies such as coronations. These collections are usually open for public view, but they are always under tight security.

Crowns and jewels are also worn by villagers and townspeople in Europe, but these are made from much less valuable materials. A brightly decorated bridal crown was traditionally the most important feature of a woman's wedding outfit. Nowadays in Denmark, the headdress of the bride has gold and silver thread embroidery, pearls, silk ribbons, and small pieces of mirror. In Germany, bridal gowns are adorned with pieces of fabric, paper, and gold leaf; sometimes flowers, glass, fruit, sheet metal, gold sequins, and glass spheres are attached.

Rings are a very popular form of jewelry in Europe. They have been used for centuries for many different purposes. From the fourteenth century on, it was popular to wear a ring in memory of a dead relative or friend, and some rings contained the hair of a loved one. Rings also could be worn as a symbol of wealth, and at funerals in Victorian Britain different types of gift rings would be given to the mourners according to their status.

Nowadays in Europe, rings are frequently given for engagements and marriages. In France, for example, "rings of faith or promise" are still given to seal the engagement between young people before their official engagement.

Gold rings from the ▶ **Thetford treasure, found in Norfolk, England, in 1976. They were made in the fourth century** A.D.

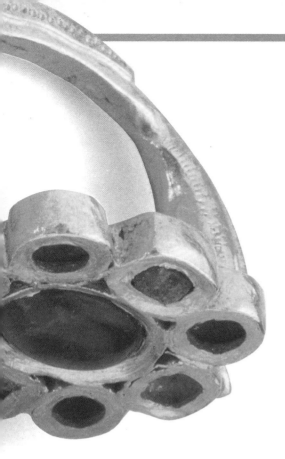

▲ **The bride and groom both wear crowns in this traditional church wedding in Rostov, southern Russia.**

Rings and other jewelry are traditionally presented as a token of love. In the Czech Republic this could be in the form of a comb, necklace, ring, or brooch. In Poland, boys used to offer beads and brooches to their sweethearts. These tokens were often made in a form that suggested love and marriage – necklaces or rings were made in the shape of hearts, clasped hands, padlocks, or Adam and Eve. You could also find the name or initials of the person and sometimes a longer inscription.

Elaborate jewelry is still worn on special occasions in the countryside in Bulgaria. Young married women wear an ornament called a *prochelnik* on their forehead or hat. Pendants known as *kabuti* are attached to the head scarf, and a chain of coins called a *podbradnik* is worn under the chin to hold a hat in place. All the best clothes and heavy silver jewelry are worn on special festivals such as Lazarouvane, the festival of youth, which takes place eight days before Easter.

These Bulgarian folksingers in national costume wear a chain called a *prochelnik* on their foreheads, a *podbradnik* chain under their chins, and an ornate gold buckle around their waists. ▶

Jewelry is also worn in Bulgaria for protection. A married woman traditionally wears a large, ornate, silver buckle around her waist to protect her abdomen when she is at work in the fields. Jewelry is also associated with magic. On the first Sunday before Lent, the peasants hold a festival that marks the beginning of spring. Here, men dress in masks and wear large, heavy, silver bells around their waists. The noise of these bells is believed to drive away evil and sickness. On St. George's Day, a bride is supposed to milk the first ewe through a ring to ensure a plentiful supply of milk for the summer. In the past, a ring was buried with the dead, as it was believed to help them on their journey to the other world. This ring also could be used to treat illness: if, for example, you had a nosebleed, you could stop it by placing the ring under your nose so that the drops of blood passed through it. In times of epidemics, Bulgarian women would wear all their metal jewelry and put a gold or silver coin in their mouths.

Although some of this jewelry still exists today, the traditions are not as strong as they were in the past. Nowadays it is only the old women who have the jewelry, which they have kept from their youth.

Jewelry sold in modern Turkey is often brilliantly colored. Gold and silver are popular, but other materials are also used. Many blue glass talismans are made and sold, both to tourists and to Turkish people, in jewelry stores and bazaars. Some of these talismans are round or oval pendants made of thick, bright blue glass, with an eye painted in the center. These are believed to protect against the evil eye. In Turkey, Bulgaria, India, and other countries around the world, people believe that an angry look or glance can cause harm or injury, especially to children. To protect them from such a look – the evil eye – people may attach amulets or charms to the clothes of babies and children.

Make a jeweled crown

You will need:
thick paper, 28 in. long, 9 in. wide
pencil
ruler
scissors
glue
glitter
foil decals
silver tinsel
red ribbons

1. Fold the paper in half lengthwise, open it up, and draw a line along the fold. Using the ruler, measure and draw six triangles down one side, as shown, and cut them out.

2. Wrap the paper around your head so that the triangles point up. Check that it fits, and cut away any excess paper.

3. Glue the glitter, tinsel, and foil decals to the paper. Glue the two ends together to create a crown, and attach the red ribbons so that they hang down at the sides.

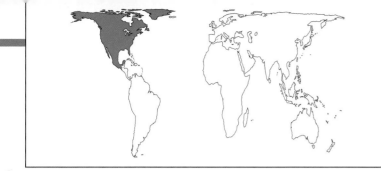

North America

Today in North America, many people wear jewelry in a similar way to Europeans. Fashionable jewelers in big cities like New York, San Francisco, and Toronto sell modern designs using expensive materials, such as gold and precious stones.

But long before Europeans arrived in North America in the sixteenth and seventeenth centuries, Native Americans had their own culture and traditions. In the 2,000-year-old burial sites of the Hopewell people, for example, jewelry made of pearls, copper, silver, and shells has been found.

When the Europeans arrived, many Native Americans were killed and others were forced to migrate. Much of the traditional culture from this period was lost or destroyed. However, some of the jewelry and decorative art forms of the past are being produced again today.

Originally, beadwork was an important form of decoration. Beads were made of local materials such as shells, grass, seeds, silver berries, or dried rosehips. Such materials were made into earrings, necklaces, and armbands. Shell beads, known as wampum, were attached to belts and costumes. Wampum was traded as money and used in special ceremonies. In some areas, beaded belts were used to send messages to other groups. Sending a white belt meant peace, but a purple belt might have meant a declaration of war. Beads were so important in Native American culture that when the Europeans first arrived they offered glass beads to the Native Americans to establish friendship.

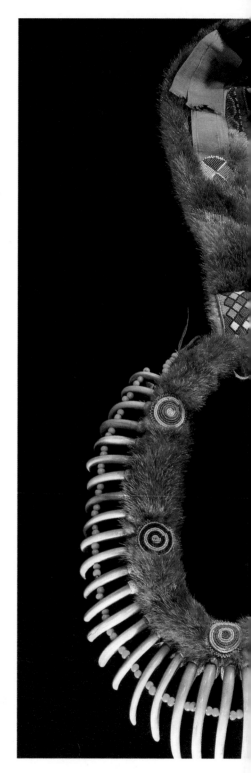

▲ This bear-claw necklace was made by the Fox people, who lived on the fringes of the Plains and Great Lakes cultures. It was worn as a mark of status, showing great bravery.

Eventually these European glass beads became more popular than shell beads and gave Native American jewelry a more colorful appearance.

Jewelry was used to indicate wealth, status, and bravery. The Blackfoot people of the northern Plains made necklaces from bear claws. These were very valuable because they indicated that the wearer was a brave hunter. Natural yellow claws were the most important and were often worn by the Blackfoot, Crow, and Western Sioux peoples. During the second half of the nineteenth century, the grizzly bear population declined because there was too much hunting, so imitation claws were carved from cow horns, hooves, and wood. Today, bear-claw necklaces are still popular, but they are made of synthetic materials such as plastic.

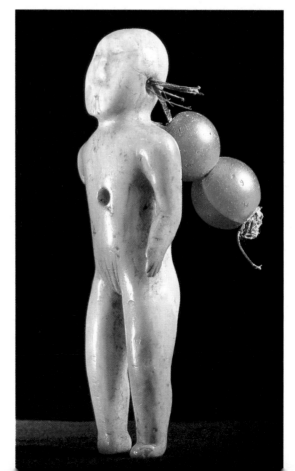

This small ivory carving ▶ of a human is decorated with blue beads and was made by the Inuit in Alaska. It was probably used as a charm and was hung around the wearer's neck.

Jewelry was traditionally worn to ▶ indicate bravery and status among Native Americans. These modern-day Shoshoni men are wearing feather headdresses and bead jewelry in a way similar to their ancestors.

The jewelry of the Sioux Indians also reflected how bravery was highly valued. Feathers were worn in the hair to show an individual's courage. A red dot painted on a feather indicated the way in which an enemy had been killed. Tufts of hair taken from the heads of enemies were attached to the arms and legs. The most stunning ornaments of all were the long feather headdresses, which sometimes reached down to the ground. They were usually made from eagle and owl feathers and were worn on ceremonial occasions. The eagle was considered a sacred animal to the Plains Indians; its feathers were prized for medicine as well as ornamentation.

Jewelry is still being made and worn by many of the Native Americans who live in the Pacific Northwest. They live close to the ocean and forest, and these places have had a major influence in their art and mythology. The raven, eagle, killer whale, shark, frog, and hawk are popular, and many clans are named after these animals. Silver and gold bracelets, necklaces, brooches, and rings are engraved with animal faces and used today by families as their crests. The raven is one of the most important figures in the mythology of the Haida Indians, whose silver bracelets often show a raven's eyes and beak. The bracelets were originally made from beaten silver coins and were worn by women as decoration. Today, these bracelets and other jewelry are made by silversmiths who may sell them commercially to tourists.

In the frozen lands of northern Canada and Alaska, the Inuit create their decorative jewelry from walrus ivory and glass beads. Both men and women wear long glass-bead earrings and lip plugs

made of ivory and stone. Traditionally, the women wore delicate ivory plugs, whereas the men wore larger plugs as they got older. Because it was uncomfortable to wear lip plugs when it was very cold, the Inuit took them out when they traveled. They would replace them when they arrived at the next village, so that they would be properly adorned. In western Alaska, headbands made from strips of fur and sheep's teeth were worn for whaling. At the center of these headbands hung a stone in the shape of a whale – a kind of good luck charm. Most Inuit jewelry is small and compact so that it can be carried easily from camp to camp. Small, functional objects, such as button fastenings, combs, and snow goggles, are also made from ivory.

The Navajo, who are the largest surviving Native American tribe, live in the Southwest near the Mexican border. They have have kept their colorful dances and ceremonies alive and have retained their traditional skills as silversmiths. They have worn fine silver jewelry since the sixteenth century, when they learned the art of silversmithing from the Mexicans. In the nineteenth century they supplied European traders with rings, bracelets, earrings, and necklaces made from silver inlaid with turquoise and other precious stones.

During the early twentieth century, traders encouraged Native Americans to produce jewelry specifically for the tourist market. Nowadays, Native American craft guilds have been set up to help maintain high standards, and Navajo silver jewelry can be found in art galleries all over the world.

For the Aztecs and Maya in Mexico, turquoise and jade were more precious than gold. The Aztecs believed that because turquoise was blue, it was like the sky and the water. Among the Maya, small balls of jade were placed in the mouths of the dead to indicate that they would go on living after death.

The Huichols live on top of the canyons in northwest Mexico. The women make bead bracelets, necklaces, pendants, and rings with very complex patterns for both men and women. The Huichol say that the patterns are given to them by their gods. Some look like the markings on a snake, and others represent sacred plants and flowers. For the Huichol, the quality of the beadwork on a piece of jewelry indicates a woman's devotion to the gods.

The Navajo Indians of the ▶ Southwest have kept their jewelry traditions alive. They are well known for their skills at making turquoise and silver bracelets, necklaces, and rings.

18

Decorate your hair with feathers

You will need:
3 feathers
red paint
paintbrush

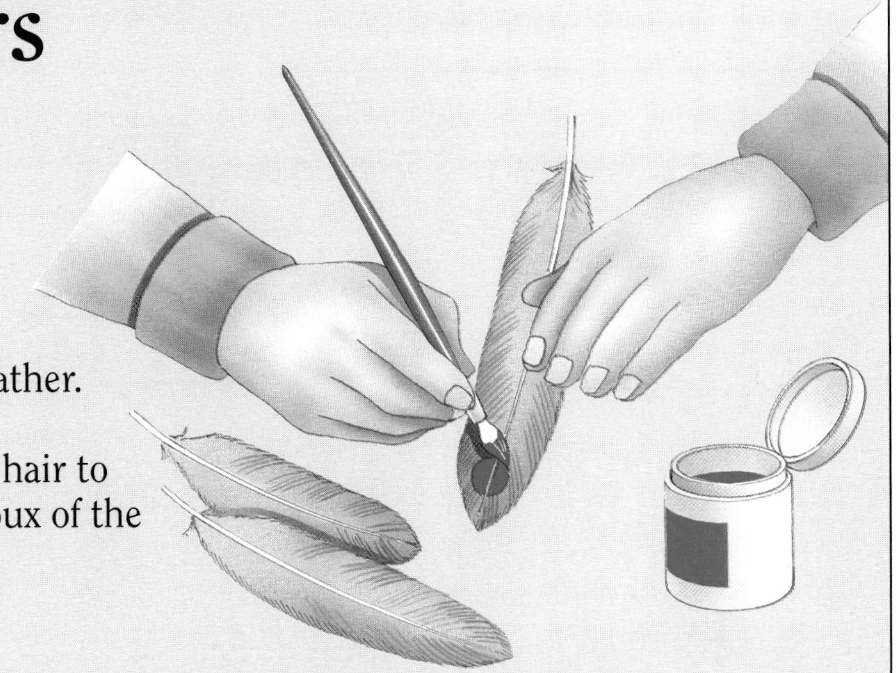

1. Paint a red dot on each feather.

2. Stick the feathers in your hair to indicate bravery, like the Sioux of the North American Plains.

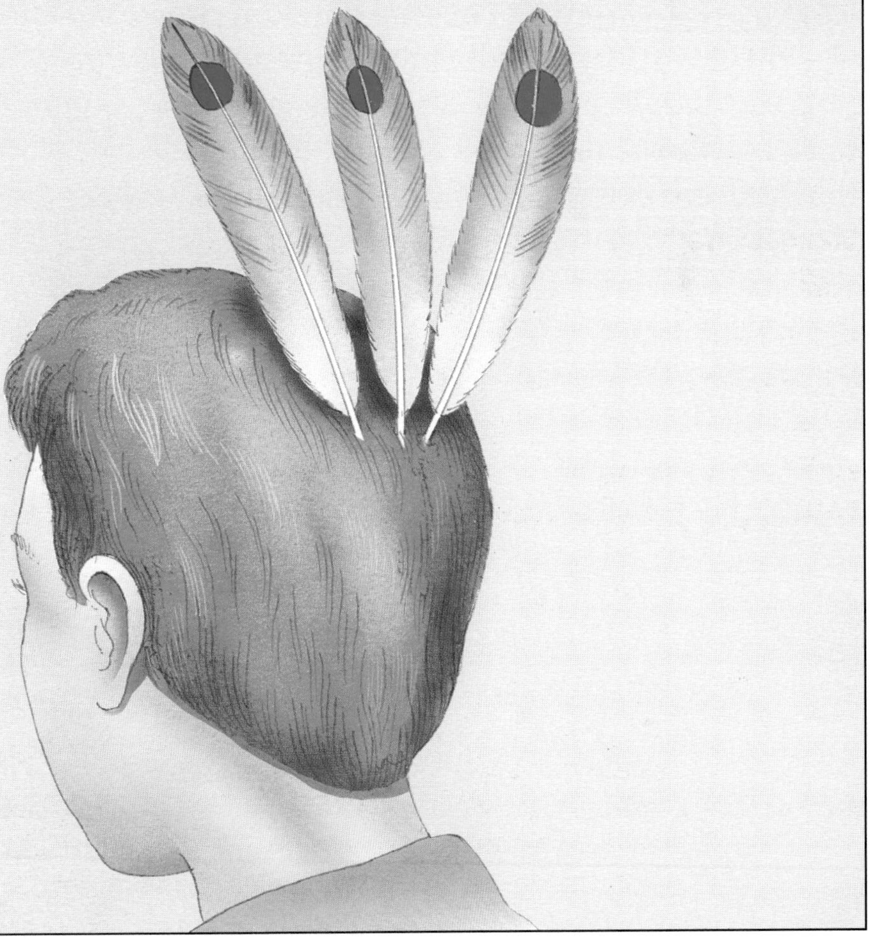

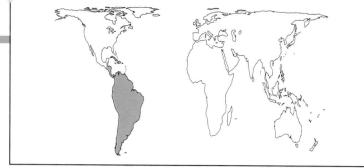

Central and South America

Long before the Spanish arrived in the sixteenth century, the Maya and Inca peoples of Central and South America enjoyed civilizations in which dress, body decoration, and art were very highly developed.

Stone carvings made by the Maya people in Central America show that the high-ranking nobles wore a great variety of costumes and ornaments. Jade was the favorite material and was used to make nose pins, ear plugs, and necklaces. Jade jewelry was often buried with the dead, and the number of jade pieces in a person's tomb was an indication of his or her wealth and importance.

Gold was an important ▶ material to the peoples of ancient Central and South America. This gold mask pendant is from the Chimu culture of Peru in the thirteenth century A.D. On either side of the face are two dragonlike animals, which were associated with status.

In ancient South America, gold was called "the sweat of the sun," while silver was "the tears of the moon." Gold was the most important material to the Incas of Peru, who associated it with their sun god, Inti. Only the ruler of the Incas was allowed to wear jewelry made of this material.

Early South American jewelry was often very colorful and made from many materials, including bright tropical birds' feathers, human hair, animal teeth, delicate fish bones, and beetle wings.

In Colombia, jewelry and precious objects have been found at the bottom of sacred lakes. At Lake Guatavita, a special ceremony used to be performed to welcome each new ruler. The old ruler was covered in gold dust and would go out on a raft and throw piles of jewelry into the lake. Sometimes he would dive into the water. The old ruler was known as El Dorado – "The Gilded Man."

When the Spanish conquered South America in the sixteenth century, the beautiful gold and jade jewelry was plundered and sometimes recast into European-style jewelry. Today, the peoples of South and Central America have lost many of their ancient traditions, but much of their jewelry is still made from feathers, skins, bones, minerals, and traded beads.

Feathers are especially important to the peoples in the Amazon rain forests in South America. They are used in headdresses to indicate the age, status, and identity of the wearer. Among the Cashinahua of eastern Peru, the most spectacular headdresses are worn for the headman's dance, which is frequently associated with fertility. Bright red macaw tail feathers, white feathers from the breast of the harpy eagle, and black turkey feathers are used. There is also a "spirit" headdress worn by dancers who imitate the spirits.

▲ A South American feather headdress from the Amazon basin.

▲ A Yanomani man carrying
feathers that he has just collected.
They will be made into jewelry.

Monkey-teeth collars are always made and worn by men. Children wear necklaces made from the teeth and bones of dangerous animals, such as the tail of the stingray, to protect themselves from attack. Other necklaces are made from animals that are admired by the Cashinahua. The ocelot is a sly and stealthy animal, and young men wear ocelot-teeth jewelry in the hope that they, too, may become cunning and successful hunters.

In other places in Central and South America, metal ornaments are popular, and silver is often used. The Araucanian people of Chile have a long history of metalworking. Large, circular pendants are worn by the headmen of a clan, and pendants, bracelets, anklets, and rings are worn by both men and women. In the Andes, a popular ornament is a metal pin known as a tapu. Tapus are elaborately decorated, and women use them to fasten their cloaks. Among the Mapuche of Chile, women often wear a chain with coins and pendants attached around the forehead and across the breast. However, when Chilean cowboys use these chains, they put them on their horses and use them as reins.

The Cashinahua wear collars around their necks made from seeds and monkey teeth. The most valuable collar is made of eight strands of monkey teeth – about 850 individual teeth. Monkeys are a very important source of food in the rain forest, and a man who has enough monkey teeth to make a collar of this size shows that he is a very good hunter.

Feathers and beads are worn as ▶ decoration among the Kayapo in Brazil. Feathers are taken from the local environment but beads, such as these blue, red, and white ones, are imported.

Asia

Since ancient times, jewelry has played an important role in the cultures of the various Asian countries. Finely polished pendants and beads more than 5,000 years old have been found in China. Jade is considered more valuable than gold or silver in China because it has always been associated with health, luck, and beauty. In ancient China, only court officials could wear belt hooks made of jade, and the tinkling of a jade ornament hanging from a belt was the sign of a gentleman.

Traditionally in China, brides would wear stunningly beautiful headdresses made of silver and gold. These were adorned with vivid blue kingfisher feathers, red flowers, butterflies, pearls, strands of red coral, and white glass beads.

Japanese women often wear wooden combs and hairpins, and brides bring their own set of combs along with them on their wedding day. It is a wedding tradition for a woman to put a comb in her hair and throw it away only if she wants a divorce. There is an ancient belief that the soul of the wearer lives between the teeth of a comb, and in Japan people think it is bad luck to pick up a comb that has been thrown away or lost.

▲ A bride from the Miao people of Taigong, China. She is wearing the traditional bridal jewelry of the Miao. Styles of headdresses are very different among the different peoples of China.

In Japan, combs and hairpins are ▶ used to show off a woman's hairstyle. In the past, women sometimes wore so many combs and pins that they had to sleep with their necks on a special pillow to keep everything in place.

◀ **Women buying bangles at a bazaar in Jodhpur, India**

In Indonesia, jewelry is associated with ▶ **magic and healing. This amulet from Borneo is used by a shaman to heal people. The shaman takes small chips of wood from the amulet and makes them into a cure.**

India is another Asian country where jewelry is very popular and has strong, symbolic ties to marriage. Traditionally, women do not always meet their husbands before marriage. If a woman wants to see what her future husband looks like, she can wear a ring with a mirror on it. At the wedding ceremony she looks down into the mirror to see his face. The bride wears as much jewelry as her family can afford, and she may not take it off for months after the wedding, as this is considered bad luck. If her husband dies, she must smash all her ornaments and remove all her jewelry.

In southern India, the husband ties a special gold pendant around the neck of his wife during the marriage ceremony to announce their union. In northern India, rural married women wear ornaments on their foreheads or noses. Some of their nose rings are so large and elaborate that they hang down over the mouth and must be lifted when the women eat.

Among Muslim and some Hindu groups, a woman who is married should not be seen in public by men who are not relatives. She wears a lot of bells on her jewelry to warn that she is approaching. The bells are also used to ward off scorpions, snakes, and evil spirits.

Jewelry is sometimes worn as an amulet in India to protect the wearer from harm. These amulets are often pendants made of silver, gold, and precious stones, but plants, animals, and cowrie shells also can be used. Some amulets are used to protect children. Jhoria-Muria boys, from Bastar in Madhya Pradesh, wear cowrie-shell ornaments all over their bodies to ward off the evil eye. Other amulets are used in India to help with love, marriage, and business.

Bangles are also very popular in India – some women wear so many bangles that they cover their entire arm. Originally, bangles were made of ivory, but nowadays, because ivory is so expensive, plastic ones are used instead. Every major town in India has a special bangle bazaar where women go to choose their bangles. The person who sells the bangles always puts them on the woman who buys them. Some bangles are so small that the woman clenches her fist and winces in pain as the bangles are pushed over her hand.

◀ This young Lisu woman from Thailand wears all her jewelry to celebrate the New Year. She wears layers of silver necklaces, some of which are made of coins. The amount of silver represents the size of her family's wealth.

In places such as Iran and Pakistan, women wear heavy and elaborate silver jewelry. Turkmen women, from northeast Iran, Turkmenistan, and northern Afghanistan, are given their jewelry by their families. The jewelry indicates their wealth and status in the community. Jewelry is worn around the head, arms, and shoulders, and some of the most ornate pieces are part of headdresses and hairstyles.

In northern Thailand and Myanmar (Burma), young Lisu women wear silver jewelry to attract men for marriage. In the villages in the evening, girls pound rice for the next day's meal, and boys may approach and talk to them. Couples exchange silver bracelets as tokens of love. The young people also organize working parties in the fields, where they wear their finest jewelry and sing songs together.

The New Year's festival is the most important ceremony in Lisu society, when all the silver jewelry is worn. The festival celebrates the turning from the old to the new, and all the silver is cleaned. On New Year's Day the women spend a long time dressing themselves in their finest silver, and they come out in the afternoon to dance and sing around the priest's tree.

Make a talisman

You will need:
shells
paints
paintbrush
string

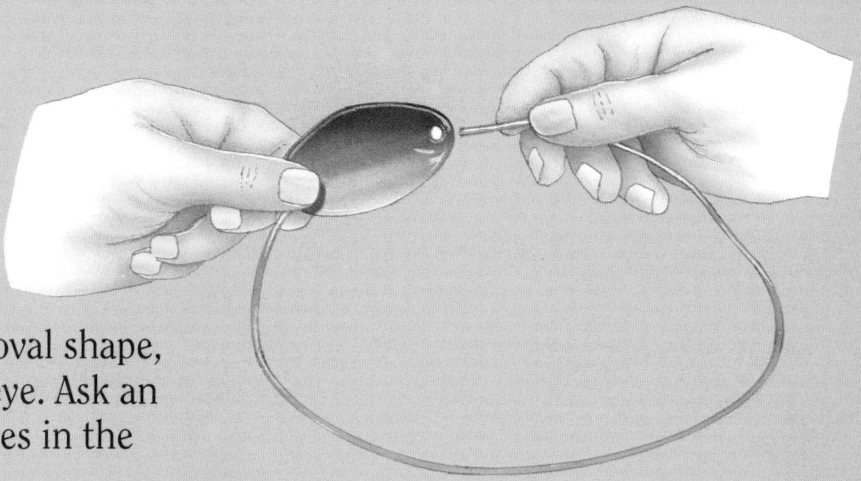

1. Choose a shell that is an oval shape, and paint it to look like an eye. Ask an adult to make two small holes in the shell, one at either end.

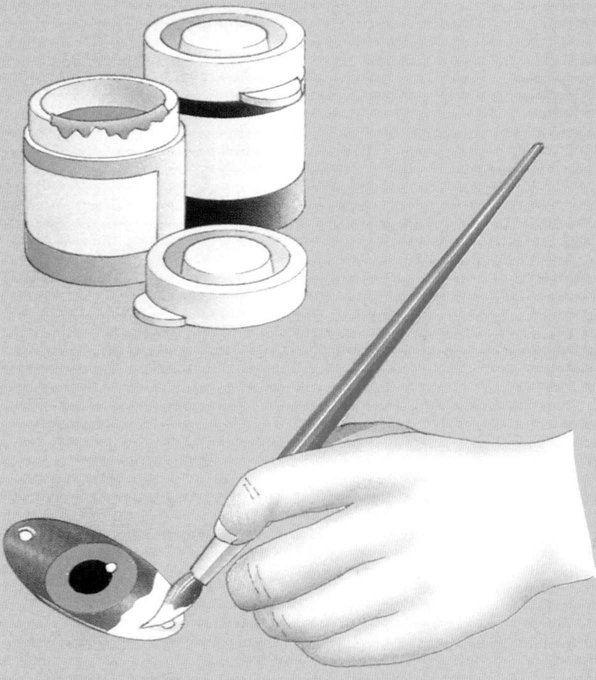

2. Measure and cut a piece of string that is long enough to go over your head and hang nicely around your neck. Remember to leave enough string to tie a knot at the back.

3. Thread the string through the holes and tie the ends together. You now have a talisman to protect you and ward off bad luck. Such pendants are often worn in India and in many other countries.

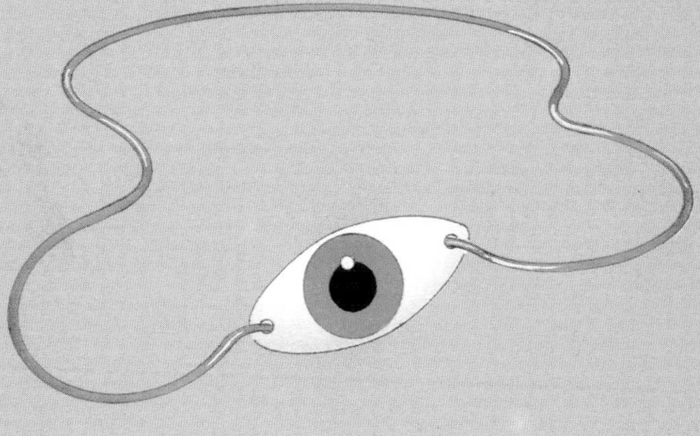

◄ **The Ifugao people in the Philippines make necklaces known as *anting-anting* from animal teeth. Young children wear them as protection from evil spirits.**

At one time in Indonesia, gold ornaments such as bracelets, anklets, and forehead ornaments were owned by the royal families and were worn at funerals by slaves. The slaves danced so much that they went into a trance and communicated with dead ancestors. This gold jewelry was said to be so powerful that if it was worn by warriors it would protect them from attack. Nowadays, gold jewelry is more associated with weddings.

Not all Indonesian jewelry is made from luxurious items. Thin branches of leathery sea coral called *akar bahar* are twisted into decorative bracelets and are said to have healing properties. In the Philippines, jewelry is also thought to cure people from sickness. When someone is ill, women perform a "curing" ceremony in which they go into a trance and wear many strings of beads. In the Andaman Islands, off the coast of India, if a person is suffering from a toothache, a necklace made of human bones is wrapped around his or her face as a cure.

Among the Naga people who live on the border of India and Myanmar, jewelry is associated with power and prestige. Naga men wear a white and black hornbill feather in dance ceremonies to show off their military achievements. One hornbill feather indicates that a man has been successful in warfare; two or more feathers mean that he is a great warrior.

The finest jewelry and ornaments are always worn at important ceremonies, such as the spring and harvest festivals. In these ceremonies, the Naga wear all their best ornaments to show that they are strong, healthy warriors. The festivals are lively events that go on for several days, with dances, feasting, drinking, and sacrifices. The men stand in a row, holding hands and dancing in their white shell skirts, brightly colored feather headdresses, and ivory bracelets.

Most Naga jewelry is made from natural materials – shells, feathers, claws, hair, tusks, and teeth. The Naga like to dye goats' hair bright red and attach this to their ornaments so that they look lively and colorful. The men used to wear large tusks as jewelry and carry long spears. The women wear necklaces and bracelets made from multicolored glass beads.

▲ **Beads are very important to the peoples of the Philippines. They are used in rituals, given as special gifts, and treasured as family heirlooms. These women's necklaces represent their wealth.**

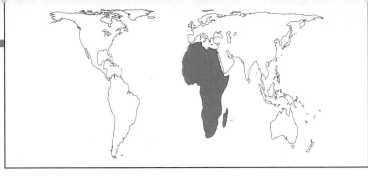

Africa

From simple beaded necklaces and ear plugs to elaborately carved ivory and gold ornaments, most African peoples wear some form of jewelry. The jewelry of Africa is a lively and ancient tradition. An oval bone pendant, found in Tunisia in north Africa, is thought to be about 15,000 years old. Among the earliest types of jewelry are beads made of ostrich-egg shells. The San women of the Kalahari Desert still thread ostrich-egg shells onto headbands and necklaces today.

In north Africa, people prefer to wear silver jewelry, which is considered purer than gold. Silver is said to have healing properties when combined with other precious stones. Topaz is believed to protect against jaundice, emeralds can help fight snake bites, and rubies are thought to be good for the heart.

In the cultures of the Sahara desert, splendid coral, brass, and ivory jewelry has been used for centuries in the kingdom of Benin (now in modern Nigeria), and gold ornamentation is popular among the Ashanti of Ghana. Benin still maintains its traditional culture. The king is called the Oba, and only he can wear a complete outfit of coral beads. A chief can wear necklaces, bracelets, and anklets made of this precious stone, but these always must be returned to the king at his death. Coral is believed to have magical and healing properties.

According to legend, one of the ancient kings of Benin took coral beads from the underwater palace of the sea god, Olokun. It is believed that when the Oba wears his coral costume, he becomes a god himself.

▲ The Oba Akenuza II of Benin in full ceremonial costume. This coral jewelry has been handed down through generations of Obas. Some pieces may be 400 years old.

The Oba and his courtiers also have fine objects made of brass. Herbs and medicines are wiped onto brass bracelets to strengthen and protect the wearer. One brass ornament is hung down from a chief's back and is called a scorpion. The shiny surface and reddish color of brass are thought to be both beautiful and threatening enough for the king and his chiefs to wear.

Ivory is also associated with royalty in the kingdom of Benin. Elaborately carved ivory bracelets are worn in special ceremonies in which the king dances. These bracelets keep his coral beads from getting tangled.

The most spectacular gold jewelry in all Africa is worn by the kings and chiefs of the Ashanti kingdom. Vast amounts of gold adorn the king and his officials. On public occasions, such as the annual Yam Festival, the king wears so much gold on his arms, wrists, and fingers that he has to rest his hands on the heads of two small boys who stand in front of him. Traditionally, slaves were forbidden to wear any jewelry, and the higher a person was in society, the more gold jewelry he or she was allowed to wear.

Recently it has become fashionable in West Africa to wear gold eyeglasses. They do not have lenses, but instead have gold wire across them. These glasses prevent the wearer from seeing easily, but they are regarded as valuable accessories.

Other metal jewelry is associated with high status. Among the Igbo of Nigeria, women wear brass circles the size of plates around their ankles. These are very heavy and make walking difficult. Because these objects are symbols of high rank, women who do not wear the anklets walk as if they are wearing them, to suggest that they are also of high status.

African women are well known for wearing brightly colored bead jewelry, especially among the Masai in Kenya and the Zulu in South Africa. There are at least forty words in the Masai language for different types of beaded decoration. The women wear their jewelry all the time, and because they are nomadic their jewelry is seen as movable wealth. Tens of thousands of tiny glass beads may be strung or sewn to make elaborate, multicolored ornaments. A woman is not considered beautiful without many layers of colorful beaded necklaces around her neck.

Masai men also wear jewelry. The warriors wear armbands and legbands, which are made by women

▲ This stiff, flat, beaded collar is worn by a Masai woman in Kenya to show that she is of marriageable age.

◄ This is the foot of Nana Owusu Sampa III, an Ashanti king from Ghana. He is wearing a gold anklet.

as a sign of love. Once the men have married they wear much less jewelry, as they have no need to attract women. But the old men always wear snuff containers, which are given to them by their eldest daughters, around their necks.

Many different objects are ▶ used to create jewelry in Africa. This Uyiyi dancer from Tanzania has strung a lightbulb around her neck to make a necklace.

Among the Zulu, beadwork is sometimes called a "language" because it is so complex and precise. Young girls sit in groups and sew beadwork love poems that they give to chosen boys. The colors and designs contain messages, and they can be read as special codes. Different stages of life are marked by different beads. When a girl falls in love, she makes a necklace of a single string of colored beads. She gives this to her lover and makes a matching set of wrist, ankle, and waist beads for herself. If you meet a group of young Zulus, you can tell who is in love with whom by the colors of the beads they wear.

Although traditional jewelry is still being made in Africa, new materials sometimes take the place of the old ones. In South Africa, discarded objects such as jar lids are used as pendants. Metal from cars is melted down and used for rings and beads. The Masai have been known to wear ear plugs made from a variety of new materials, including rolled-up newspapers, plastic, bottles, and buttons.

You will need:
a box of ziti
many different-
  colored paints
paintbrush
string
scissors

Make anklets, bracelets, and necklaces

1. Paint the pasta many different colors.

2. Measure how much string is needed to make anklets, bracelets, and necklaces to fit you, and cut these lengths. Remember to always leave enough string to tie a knot at the back, and make sure the string for the necklace is quite loose so that you can take it on and off easily.

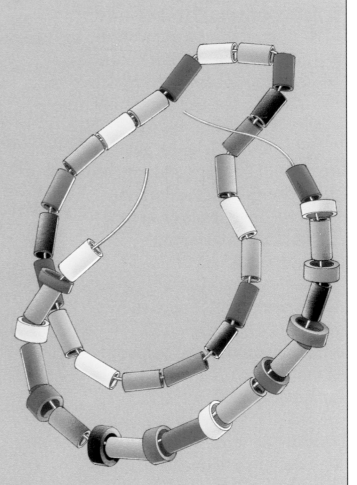

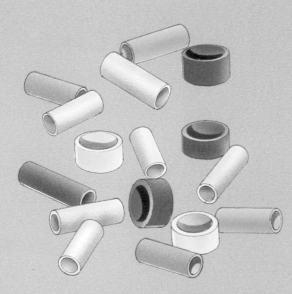

3. Thread the painted ziti onto the different pieces of string and tie a knot at the end. You can then put as many layers as you like around your neck, arms, and ankles.

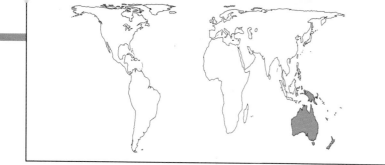

The Pacific

Many different types of jewelry and ornamentation are worn by the peoples of the Pacific region. For centuries, valuable goods have been traded from one island to the next, and sometimes jewelry is exchanged as money. In the Solomon Islands, shell belts are used to buy pigs and canoes. The more shell belts a person owns, the higher his or her status. On special ceremonial occasions the belts are worn for everyone to see.

In fact, shells are used in much of the jewelry and ornamentation of the Solomon Islands. Head ornaments called *kapkap* are made of a cream-colored giant clam shell disk. Delicate, dark brown tortoise-shell designs are fixed to the clam shell and the *kapkap* is then attached to the forehead with a headband made of fiber.

Armbands such as this one from Papua New Guinea are made from pigs' tusks, and are worn by men as decoration and as a sign of wealth. ▶

In Fiji, ivory from the sperm whale and pearl-shell disks are worn as pendants and act as special badges to show status. In this culture, a golden cowrie shell can be worn only by men of high rank.

On the Trobriand Islands and other islands near Papua New Guinea, two types of shell jewelry are used as money as well as for decoration. Men wear armbands known as *mwali,* and women wear a *soulava,* or shell necklace. These two ornaments act as currency in an exchange system called the *kula.* Armbands are exchanged only for necklaces, which means that they circulate from person to person and island to island in a counterclockwise direction. The necklaces circulate in the opposite direction. The *mwali* and *soulava* are worn temporarily to show status. Some pieces of jewelry have become famous. They have names and myths that describe where they have traveled.

It is not only shell ornaments that are worn to show status in Pacific cultures. Traditionally, brightly colored feathers were traded between islands and they, too, have become highly valued. In New Zealand, high-ranking Maoris stuck feathers in their hair and secured them with wooden combs. Some of these feathers were from birds that are now extinct. They were considered so rare that special wooden boxes were carved to store the feathers in, and they were passed on from generation to generation.

Elaborately carved Maori jade breast ornaments called *hei-tiki* were also passed on as heirlooms. Sometimes the *hei-tiki* were buried with the owner and then dug up again and worn by the grandchild. These ornaments were more frequently worn by women than men, and the wife of a captured chief always had to send her *hei-tiki* to the wife of his captor.

The most elaborate and competitive display of ornamentation exists among the highland peoples of Papua New Guinea. One of the groups is the Wahgi, who live in the foothills on either side of a valley. For a few months every year, all the different clans come together for a pig feast. This ceremony is very competitive. The clans perform in front of crowds of spectators and show off their decorations. If a warrior clan is not very beautifully adorned, it is believed that the clan may lose its next battle. The men hope that their decoration will be good enough to attract women. They wear long, black bird plumes called Stephanie Tails on their heads, and the dancers help one another prepare before the dance. Jingling pearl shells are hung from the men's belts. Armbands and other jewelry are added.

Nowadays the Wahgi use many modern objects for jewelry. Some women wear jar lids instead of shells as forehead

▲ This *hei-tiki* was made in the eighteenth century and was given as a gift to a missionary. Among the Maori, *hei-tikis* were said to have special powers.

ornaments, and beer bottle caps are used as earrings. Only the older men still wear elaborate shell ornaments, while younger men push cash notes through their armbands to decorate them. Pink bubble-gum wrappers and red sardine can labels are sometimes added to headbands and wigs.

The Australian Aborigines have also adapted their traditional decorations. Small pieces of oval pearl shells were used in some places as forehead ornaments, but nowadays jar lids may be used instead.

The men and women of Melville Island, off the northern coast of Australia, sometimes wear rows of bangles woven from human hair and decorated with seeds or feathers. These are worn as signs of mourning, particularly for an important or well-liked person.

◀ Feathers are seen as very valuable by many Pacific peoples. This dancer is from Port Moresby, Papua New Guinea.

In central Australia, pearl shell ornaments called *lonka lonka* are used as charms to attract women. The man sings to the shell, asking lightning to enter it. Later, he ties the shell to his waistband and dances with it on. The woman he wishes to attract will see the lightning flashing on the *lonka lonka* and be attracted to the man.

The use of hair and teeth is widespread in the jewelry of the Pacific. Human hair is used to attach pearl shell disks in the Marquesas Islands. In Samoa, a headdress known as a *tuinga* was worn by noble families on festive occasions and by chiefs in times of war.

This was made of bleached human hair on barkcloth, decorated with feathers, and with a band of shells on the forehead.

In Tahiti and other islands, sharks' teeth and dogs' hair were included in decorative breast ornaments. The male dancers in Hawaii wore boar-tusk bracelets and bands of fiber with dogs' teeth on their legs. Sometimes as many as one thousand such teeth were used.

But perhaps the most unusual form of decoration was used by the Maori of Taronki. They would thrust the beaks of live birds into holes in their earlobes and wear them as ornaments. You could call this living jewelry!

In Papua New Guinea, ▶ men wear jewelry and decoration to show their status and power. Feathers, shells, beads, and grasses may be used to create the decoration.

44

Make a necklace from recycled materials

You will need:
4 toilet paper tubes
scissors
aluminum foil
candy wrappers
glue
string
newspaper
different-colored paints
paintbrush

1. Cut each toilet roll into three smaller rolls and cover the pieces with foil. Glue the candy wrappers to the foil.

2. Measure how much string is needed to create a necklace. Remember to leave plenty of string for tying a knot, and to make the necklace loose enough to take it on and off.

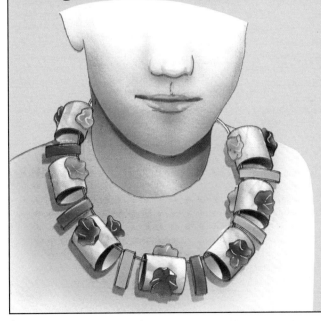

3. Thread the string through the tubes and tie the ends in a knot.

4. Cut thin strips of newspaper. Paint them different colors and let them dry. Wrap the strips around the string between the toilet paper roll tube sections. Glue their ends together to make hanging loops.

You can use many other types of recycled materials to decorate your necklace, such as egg cartons, yogurt cup lids and peanut shells.

Glossary

Amulet An object used to protect a person or to ward off evil spirits.

Anglo-Saxons People from Germany who settled in Britain in the fifth century A.D.

Anklet An ornament that is worn around the ankle.

Barkcloth A type of cloth made from the bark of a tree.

Bazaar A market or street of small stalls popular in the Middle East and Asia.

Bronze Age A period of human culture characterized by the use of bronze tools. It began in Europe around 3500 B.C. and in western Asia and Egypt somewhat earlier.

Clan A group of families with a common ancestor or surname.

Coronation A ceremony for crowning a king or queen.

Courtiers Attendants at court.

Cowrie A white shell found in Africa, Asia, and the Pacific and used for decoration and as money.

Crest The symbol of a family or clan.

Epidemic A disease that affects many people in a community or area.

Evil eye A look or glance believed to cause great harm, especially to young children or babies.

Guild A club or organization that is set up to help craftspeople.

Heirlooms Any objects that have been in a family for generations.

Hindu A follower of the main Indian religion, Hinduism.

Hornbill A bird from Africa and Asia that has a very large beak.

Inlaid Objects or jewels set in the surface of a piece of jewelry or furniture.

Inscription A signature or sentence carved or engraved onto a coin or piece of jewelry.

Iron Age The period of human culture characterized by the smelting of iron and its almost universal use in industry beginning around 1000 B.C. in southern Europe and somewhat earlier in western Asia and Egypt.

Jade A semiprecious stone that varies in color from white to green and that can be polished to a high sheen.

Macaw A large tropical parrot from South America that has a long tail and brightly colored feathers.

Migrate To move from one place or country and settle in another.

Mourning Feelings or actions that show a person's sadness after someone's death.

Muslim A follower of the religion of Islam.

Mythology A group of myths associated with a particular culture.

Nomadic Describes people who move from place to place to find land for their animals and to grow food.

Oba The title of the kings in Benin, West Africa.

Ocelot A jaguar-like animal with a dark-spotted brown coat that lives in Central and South America.

Plumage Layers of feathers covering a bird's body.

Plundered Stolen.

Prestige A person's status or rank in society.

Rank A person's official position within a society or organization.

Recast To melt a metal object down and reshape it into something else.

Rosehip The berry-like fruit of a rose.

Snuff Fine tobacco powder for sniffing up the nose.

Status A person's position within a society or organization.

Surreal Unreal or dreamlike.

Synthetic Made from artificial or unnatural materials.

Talisman An object that has magical or protective powers.

Trance A dreamlike state.

Vikings Danish, Norwegian, and Swedish people who lived in Europe in the eighth to eleventh centuries A.D.

Books to Read

Caldecott, Barrie. *Jewelry Crafts*. Fresh Start. New York: Franklin Watts, 1992.

Jackson, Julia A. *Gemstones: Treasures from the Earth's Crust*. Earth Resources. Hillside, NJ: Enslow Publishers, 1989.

Rosen, Mike. *Summer Festivals*. Seasonal Festivals. New York: Bookwright Press, 1991.

Information about individual cultures may also be found in the 48-volume Cultures of the World series by Marshall Cavendish Corporation (North Bellmore, NY), or in your library's encyclopedia.

Index

The jewelry and accessories in this book come from many different peoples. Various types of jewelry and accessories are listed in the index, such as "necklaces," "anklets," and "rings." If you want to see how jewelry and accessories are used, look at entries such as "ceremonies" and "festivals." You can use the "peoples" entry to look up jewelry and accessories from the cultures mentioned in this book.